Love, Lessons, & Resilience
Poetry From The Soul

TANYA "TRINITY" HOLLAND

Love, Lessons, & Resilience
Poetry From the Soul

Tanya "Trinity" Holland

Pearly Gates Publishing, LLC, Harlem, GA (USA)

Love, Lessons, & Resilience:
Poetry From the Soul

Copyright © 2022
Tanya "Trinity" Holland

All Rights Reserved.
In accordance with the U.S. Copyright Act of 1976, the scanning, uploading, and electronic sharing of any part of this book without the author's or publisher's permission is unlawful piracy and theft of the author's intellectual property. If you would like to use material from this book (other than brief quotations for literary reviews), we ask you to please cite your reference.
Thank you for your support of the author's rights.

Paperback ISBN 13: 978-1-948853-50-7
Digital IBSN 13: 978-1-948853-51-4
Library of Congress Control Number: 2022908293

Scripture references are taken from the King James Version (KJV) and New International Version (NIV) of The Holy Bible and used with permission from Zondervan via BibleGateway.com. Public Domain.

Pearly Gates Publishing, LLC
Angela Edwards, CEO
P.O. Box 639
Harlem, GA 30814
BestSeller@PearlyGatesPublishing.com

What Others Are Saying...

"Tanya and I have known each other since childhood. I have watched and experienced her growth from a young girl to the woman she is today. We have shared life's precious moments, including becoming mothers to the tragedy of losing parents. Her poetry speaks from all of her life experiences and a deep place within her soul. It amazes me how the words just flow from her, as poetry is truly her gift."

LYLAS (Love You Like A Sis)
Victoria Wested ~ Lifelong Friend and Soul Sister

🦋 🦋 🦋 🦋 🦋

"Tanya's poetry comes from a place deep within her. She shares her experiences, allowing her emotions to spring to life in her work. She makes you feel like you are experiencing what is being said, whether it is love, joy, sadness, happiness, freedom, or even shame. Tanya's words hit you in your heart, leaving you better after reading or hearing her words."

Wendi Hammond ~ Friend, Soul Sister, and Evangelist

🦋 🦋 🦋 🦋 🦋

"I have been one of Tanya's biggest fans for more than 30 years. Her words—whether written or spoken—have always been mindful. She always strives to be the best version of herself. She is selfless in sharing her life's lessons with those she cares about, which resonates in her poetry. I am honored and grateful to call her my friend and Soul Sister, as she means the world to me. I am so proud of her accomplishments."

With Much Love, **Aleja Estronza**

Dedications & Acknowledgments

First and foremost, I give all glory and honor to my Heavenly Father for His love, grace, mercy, and the gifts of written and spoken word.

This book is dedicated to my sister-friends who have held my hand, loved me when I didn't love myself, cried with me and dried my tears, told me to get back in the game of life when I thought I had lost, and most importantly, always reminded me that I am worthy. Thank you and boundless love to: Vicki, Wanda, Aleja, Wendi, Cindy, Darla, Maryanne, and Jenean. I would rather have all of you help carry me through this life than the ones carrying my casket!

I also dedicate this book to my son, Christopher. Without you, my life would not have a purpose. Thank you for loving me, understanding me, never giving up on me, and for being such an amazing person. You and Karen bring so much love and light to this world. I love you both with all my heart!

To my Holland family... And Still, We Rise!!! I LOVE YOU ALL!

Preface

As a teenager growing up in a dysfunctional family, I didn't know who to talk to when I needed to get things off my chest. Most often, I was in a dark, lonely place, and music, a pen, and a piece of paper were my therapy. The words "I love you" weren't used very often, and they weren't spoken that much in my home. Survival was my daily mindset. I knew my friends wouldn't understand because their lives seemed so normal.

I found myself excelling at being the comedic relief, the life of the party, and the flirty girl—all while my soul was dying on the inside. My silent prayers and a blank piece of paper were the only things hearing my cries. Unfortunately, all the poetry from those times in my life were lost in a basement flood, except for a couple I managed to salvage.

When I became a young woman and a single mother at a young age, my self-esteem, self-worth, and self-value were nonexistent...with no recovery in sight. I thought making myself desirable would boost my self-confidence or being "Miss Independent" would make me more of a catch. Neither worked. Instead, the wrong men gravitated toward me and entered my life for the wrong reasons, leaving my vulnerable heart crushed. When my spirit could take no more and I was barely clinging to hope, losing faith, and falling back into the darkness again, I returned to my old friends, prayer, and my pen and paper.

I began to write again—this time, with the guidance of the Holy Spirit.

This literary journey began a little over 20 years ago. *Love, Lessons, & Resilience* was written with the hope that other young women who think they're not worthy, pretty enough, smart enough, kind enough, good enough, or even unlovable will be inspired to see they are conquerors! Some who read this book may feel like they have lost their voice due to domestic abuse or the embarrassment of feeling like a victim of that abuse. Baby girl, it wasn't your fault! No one deserves to be treated like an outlet for someone's anger issues or a pawn for their need to control and play mind games.

Without a doubt, I know I wouldn't have been ready to finish this book had I not gone through some of the trials I endured. I've bounced back and am now sharing my gift with the world. Baby girl, you will bounce back, too!

My prayer is that *Love, Lessons, & Resilience* inspires women to heal, grow, and know that with God, all things are truly possible. His timing is always perfect.

~ Trinity ~

Tanya "Trinity" Holland

Floetry: "My Apology"

"Growth, I released my grief, it was a heavy load.
Survived the sleep and now, I'm letting go.
Waking up and living up to what I had proposed.
Woman now, I love the girl I used to be.
Every step she took was reaching out to me.
Every breath is blessed responsibility.
We made it, baby!"

From the album *Flo'Ology* (2005), Geffen Records
Songwriters: Natalie Stewart, Scott Spencer, and Marsha Ambrosius

Love, Lessons, & Resilience: Poetry From the Soul

Table of Contents

What Others Are Saying... vi
Dedications & Acknowledgments vii
Preface viii
Floetry: "My Apology" x
Cocoon 1
Psalm 91 2
Love 3
    The Seed 4
    For Love 5
    Day Dreamin' 8
    New Boo Junkie 9
    Letting Go 10
    Together We 12
    Again 14
    Luke 18:15-17 16
    1 Corinthians 13 17
Lessons 18
    Lessons 19
    Romans 8:38-39 22
    Weakness 23
    2 Corinthians 12:9-10 25
    Living Will 26
    The Carpet 28
    Matthew 19:6 29
    Repenting 30

- 1 John 1:9 ... 31
- Acts 3:19 ... 32
- Luke 15:10 ... 33
- Lost ... 34
- Drowning ... 35
- Matthew 7:7 ... 37
- You Are Needed ... 38
- Perfect ... 39
- John 15:12,16-17 ... 40

Resilience ... 41
- Rear View ... 42
- More to Me ... 43
- Nations ... 45
- Tragically Beautiful ... 46
- Allowance ... 47
- Give It to Me ... 49
- Isaiah 41:10 ... 51
- The Mourning ... 52
- Ephesians 4:22-24 ... 53
- Resilience ... 54
- Matthew 5:14-16 ... 55
- James 1:12 ... 56
- Madness ... 57
- Matthew 6:33 ... 60

About the Author ... 61

Cocoon

You kept this fragile life protected,
Wrapped in Your precious love.
You held me in Your hands
And kept me secured.
Like the butterfly in its cocoon,
You kept me there inside.
Each day, I would fight to survive,
But You kept Your hands gently around me—
Not letting go until You knew
That I would be ready.
You let me struggle and fight,
But You wouldn't let go
Until You knew that I would be okay.
You kept people from coming in
Who would try to undo the work within.
You only allowed those to come close
Who would help mature my spiritual growth.
Then, the day came when the sun was shining bright,
And the wind was just right.
You knew my wings were ready,
And my spirit and soul
Had matured, and I became steady.
I was calm in my cocoon
But You knew it was time,
And You whispered in my ear,
"It's time for you to fly.
You are strong enough to do this on your own.
Now, go...fly...shine your light,
And tell the world about the love you found."

Tanya "Trinity" Holland

Psalm 91

"He that dwelleth in the secret place of the most High shall abide under the shadow of the Almighty. I will say of the Lord, He is my refuge and my fortress: my God; in him will I trust. Surely he shall deliver thee from the snare of the fowler, and from the noisome pestilence. He shall cover thee with his feathers, and under his wings shalt thou trust: his truth shall be thy shield and buckler. Thou shalt not be afraid for the terror by night; nor for the arrow that flieth by day; Nor for the pestilence that walketh in darkness; nor for the destruction that wasteth at noonday. A thousand shall fall at thy side, and ten thousand at thy right hand; but it shall not come nigh thee. Only with thine eyes shalt thou behold and see the reward of the wicked. Because thou hast made the Lord, which is my refuge, even the most High, thy habitation; There shall no evil befall thee, neither shall any plague come nigh thy dwelling. For he shall give his angels charge over thee, to keep thee in all thy ways. They shall bear thee up in their hands, lest thou dash thy foot against a stone. Thou shalt tread upon the lion and adder: the young lion and the dragon shalt thou trample under feet. Because he hath set his love upon me, therefore will I deliver him: I will set him on high, because he hath known my name. He shall call upon me, and I will answer him: I will be with him in trouble; I will deliver him, and honour him. With long life will I satisfy him, and shew him my salvation."

For the Professor ~ My Daddy

Thank you for believing in me when I didn't believe in myself. You helped mold me into the woman I am today, and, because of you, the world heard my poetry for the first time. For that, I will be forever grateful. There would be no me without you. I know in my heart that you would be proud to say,
"That's my Baby Girl!"
Rest in Paradise, Daddy.

Love Always,
Your Baby Girl

Love

Because a young woman fell in love through rose-colored glasses...

Tanya "Trinity" Holland

The Seed

I'm giving you a seed.
This is no ordinary seed;
It is as different
As you and I,
But it will grow, as all seeds do.
Take this seed—as small as it may be—
And bury it with tenderness.
Shower it with patience.
Be kind, and you'll feel it grow.
Be unkind, and it will wither.
Respect what it represents,
And you'll see it change and bloom.
Take good care and be gentle,
For it is new and fragile.
For this seed is a symbol
Of the friendship and love
We have for each other.
And like a seed,
It will blossom
Into something beautiful
And unique—
As unique as you and I,
But as amazing as the blossom
That once was a seed.

For Love

Something in my life
That there has been a lack of.
Although I get plenty of love
From my family and friends,
It isn't always enough
To fill this void.
This need and desire
Will not be ignored.
Joy and happiness,
Friendship and companionship
Are the only things
That can absorb this loneliness.
I think I have paid my dues,
But with all that I have paid,
I still own these blues.
My empty heart waits
And anticipates
The day when it will be filled
With the unconditional love
Of a man with a strong will,
To restore this spirit
Which others have managed to kill.
But I hold no grudge;
I left my baggage in the past.
But this need just won't budge.
For Love...
I know it so well.
I have given so much.
How much, only my heart can tell.
With all that I have given,
I still have so much left.
But there is no one here
Who I can share my love with.
This mind, body, and spirit

Tanya "Trinity" Holland

Have been used and abused,
But still, I refuse
To give up on love.
My heart beats it.
My lungs breathe it.
My body aches
From all that it takes.
So, patiently I wait
For love...
The one that only
God can create.
He knows what I need
In my soulmate.
My soul grows tired;
I don't know how long
I can subdue this fire.
For love...
So, I continue to move,
Not missing a step,
Keeping up with my groove.
My body constantly busy.
My mind becomes dizzy
From all the coming and going
Throughout my hectic day.
And at the end of all the running,
I fall into my bed,
Exhausted mind and muscles aching,
Feeling half-dead.
That's when reality hits me,
Painfully reminding me
As I lay there in the darkness,
That there is no one there—
Just the piercing emptiness
Of my cold, lonely bed.
The only source of comfort
Is the sound of my beating heart,

Which seems to beat out of rhythm,
Needing to stay in time with him.
But there is no him.
So, until then,
Jesus keeps my heart's pace
As I lay there through the night.
I ask,
What did I ever do
To suffer this plight?
I always tried to treat people right.
I know I am far from perfect
And that I have done my share of dirt,
Not meaning to inflict any hurt.
But still, I wait
For love...
I've had my share
Of love in the past,
But all of those would not last.
Wrong timing and bad decisions:
I can no longer deal
With this inquisition.
I just want someone
To accept me for me,
With all my faults
And the end result.
Still, I wait
For love...

Tanya "Trinity" Holland

Day Dreamin'

Braids, dreads, bald heads...
That cocoa-brown skin that sweats like honey
And is softer than the finest silk.
Full, luscious, soft lips
That make me quiver with every tender kiss.
I love my Black man.
Firm body, tight booty;
Thugged-out or business-suited down,
Doo-rag or a baseball cap
Pulled down—almost hiding your eyes.
The eyes that make my heart melt
Whenever you look into mine.
I love my Black man.
Strong arms from holding off the world.
Strong spirit that keeps you goin'.
Powerful legs from carrying the weight of this world.
And a kind and patient heart made for loving your family.
I have seen your struggle
And felt your hidden tears.
Let me gently rub away your pain.
I love my Black man.
Indecisive and unwilling at times,
You're just trying to grow
In this corrupt soil
Fertilized with ignorance
With no seeds to sow.
Let my love and compassion rain down on you
So that I can watch you grow
Healthy roots that will hold up this family tree—
The one that grew from you and me.
I Love My Black Man!

New Boo Junkie

Hello, NBA! My name is Trinity,
And I am a New Boo Junkie.
You know when you see that someone new
Who could possibly be your New Boo?
When the butterflies start to brew,
The next thing you know,
I'm saying, "Hey, Boo! What's good with you?"
The conversation starts to flow
And he begins the New Boo voodoo
That only the New Boos know how to do.
Then baby, you have no clue
The things I got cookin'
In my bowl of emotional stew.
You're going to have me
Stuck to you like glue.
Yes, I'm all up in this
Brand New Boo Junkie dew.
He's got me tingling from
The top of my head
All the way down to my
You know who.
Just the simple view of you
Makes a girl want to forget
All the things she has to do
Just to be close to you.
Girl, shake it off.
This is all too new.
You can't keep jumping
From New Boo to New Boo.

Hello! My name is Trinity,
And I am a New Boo Junkie.
That's why I'm here
At the NBA—New Boo Anonymous.

Letting Go

I want to let go
And give away,
But my mind won't let me.
It constantly reminds me
Of all the hurt and pain,
Although I feel with you
I can finally let go.
But then there are those things
That remind me
You are not alone.
Those things that keep me grounded,
But my heart keeps on pounding
For the love of you.
If only I could let go
Of all the things in my past,
Maybe my heart
Could learn to love at last.
But love has always been
A hurting thing.
That's why it is hard to bring
My feelings to the surface.
Then, there are the times
When I can't hold them back.
They come rushing in;
My emotions then attack.
My mouth starts to tell
Things that only my heart can feel.
I try to stop.
By then, it's too late.
The feelings I have been trying to hide
Finally escape.
My mind keeps telling me,
"No, don't let those feelings go!"
But as the days go by,

I slowly become
No longer afraid
Of what my heart feels.
I am truly amazed
That just the simple thought of you
Can make my eyes fill
With that emotional dew.
I keep telling myself to wait.
My heart anxiously anticipates
Letting go,
And tell you what you already know
By the way that I am
When we are together.
The way I touch you...
The way I kiss you...
All those things give it away.
My heart has gone astray,
And for the first time in my life,
I KNOW that it is okay
To finally
LET GO...

Tanya "Trinity" Holland

Together We...

You are in my life for a reason,
Whether it be for love
Or just a season.
You are someone I can learn and grow from—
From this life to kingdom come.
We are spiritually connected
And divinely guided.

Together we...
Together we...

Flow together, like wind and rain.
When I am with you, I feel no pain.
You are my motivation,
My eternal inspiration.
You breathe the air I breathe.
You share this time and space with me.
Your touch reveals
Things I thought
I could no longer feel.

Together we...
Together we...

Are like new flowers in Spring.
Who knows what this newness will bring?
In my heart I know
You are here to heal and soothe
My raging soul,
And teach and show me things
Far beyond my physical being.

Together we...
Together we...

Are like waves crashing from the ocean,
Each with its own rhythm
Filled with emotion.
You are my Aquarian
That carries my Piscean waters
Of enlightened energy and
Intellectual superiority.

Together we...
Together we...

Are like stars in the night sky,
Shining our light
On others' darkness;
Touching people's lives
When they are filled with sadness.

Together we...
Together we...

Are like one,
Under God's beautiful sun.

The following is dedicated to a parent's love and prayer to end gun violence.

Again

Damn! Not again!
She was only two,
And last week, he was only five.
I don't even want to know
What's going to happen next week
Or even tomorrow or tonight.
This just ain't right.
They're just babies,
And it was just a stupid snowball fight.
I saw the other little girl
Who now walks with a limp,
And she just turned ten.
Why does this keep happening
Again and Again?
All because someone
Felt like they got dissed.
He just wanted to play ball
In the park,
Now he's left with a permanent mark
Just because someone had to prove a point.
Baby girl had a future,
Headed off to college to be a doctor.
She didn't get to see her graduation
Because homeboy
Needed to make his gang initiation.
I look at my son
And pray to God that the devil
Doesn't take another innocent one.
The little baby lying in the carriage
Just had his christening—
And not a moment too soon;

Now, Jesus carries him to Heaven.
The sadder part to that
Is the person they arrested
Was only eleven.
What is happening to this world?
Our kids just can't be
Normal boys and girls.
I just hope
When they go before the court
That the judge asks them,
"Do you remember being five?
Kissing your first girl
Or learning how to drive?
Well, that little person's life you took
Won't even get to read their first book."
And with that, she will give you life.
But your greatest day will come
When your life is over and done,
And you stand before the Creator.
I wonder what you will have to say then.
I pray this doesn't happen...
Again.

Tanya "Trinity" Holland

Luke 18:15-17

"People were also bringing babies to Jesus for Him to place His hands on them. When the disciples saw this, they rebuked them. But Jesus called the children to Him and said, 'Let the little children come to Me, and do not hinder them, for the kingdom of God belongs to such as these. Truly I tell you, anyone who will not receive the kingdom of God like a little child will never enter it.'"

1 Corinthians 13

"If I speak in the tongues of men or of angels, but do not have love, I am only a resounding gong or a clanging cymbal. If I have the gift of prophecy and can fathom all mysteries and all knowledge, and if I have a faith that can move mountains, but do not have love, I am nothing. If I give all I possess to the poor and give over my body to hardship that I may boast, but do not have love, I gain nothing. Love is patient, love is kind. It does not envy, it does not boast, it is not proud. It does not dishonor others, it is not self-seeking, it is not easily angered, it keeps no record of wrongs. Love does not delight in evil but rejoices with the truth. It always protects, always trusts, always hopes, always perseveres. Love never fails. But where there are prophecies, they will cease; where there are tongues, they will be stilled; where there is knowledge, it will pass away. For we know in part, and we prophesy in part, but when completeness comes, what is in part disappears. When I was a child, I talked like a child, I thought like a child, I reasoned like a child. When I became a man, I put the ways of childhood behind me. For now we see only a reflection as in a mirror; then we shall see face to face. Now I know in part; then I shall know fully, even as I am fully known. And now these three remain: faith, hope and love.
But the greatest of these is love.

·

Lessons

What she learned after she took off the rose-colored glasses...

Lessons

Tight shirts, short skirts,
Long hair and makeup just right,
High heels and those long, manicured nails.
All these things I thought
Made me a woman
Without fail; anything to catch a man's eye…
And that I did.
Not only did I catch his eye,
I caught his disease with a lifelong bid.

LESSON ONE
Tell him your dreams.
Let him know who you are.
Dazzle him with big words
And melt his heart.
Do all the little things
That make him feel special,
When the only thing you're really making
Is a baby.

LESSON TWO
Not good enough to marry
But good enough to screw.
I know there's more to me
Than just a piece of ass to you.
So, play hard to get.
Don't give in so quick.
Only tell him what he needs to know.
Keep your answers short
And make 'em stick.
Keep him guessin',
When all the while, he's out messin'
With everything that walks with a sway
And everybody's got something to say.

LESSON THREE
Get yourself together.
Set off on your own.
This time, let no one
Stop you from growin'.
But wait—there it is again.
That voice...you know the one
That used to make you scream and moan.
So, I tell myself,
"It's better than being alone!
This time, it's on MY terms."
The next thing you know,
He's got me
Running his errands,
Cleaning his house,
Cooking his meals,
Doing his laundry,
Paying HIS bills.

STOP!

LESSON FOUR
Enough is enough.
I can't take any more.
I left more than him
When I walked out that door.
I left behind a person
Who wasn't me
To finally find something...
Something deep inside of me.
That something that's been missing
Since Lesson One;
The love from within
That will never be undone.
Although I've learned from each
Of these lessons,

I seem to have forgotten
The unconditional love
That is God's blessing
That has been here
Through each and every lesson.

Tanya "Trinity" Holland

Romans 8:38-39

"For I am convinced that neither death nor life, neither angels nor demons, neither the present nor the future, nor any powers, neither height nor depth, nor anything else in all creation, will be able to separate us from the love of God that is in Christ Jesus our Lord."

Weakness

I kept telling myself
I wouldn't let you back in.
Then, I let my guard down
Once again
And allowed you to work your way
Back into my heart.
I wish you didn't know
My weakness from the start,
That my loneliness was like a demon.
I wish I never shared with you
The things from deep within,
Because after all,
I never thought
You would use them against me.
You infiltrated my defenses
That took a lifetime to build,
And then you abandoned me—
Leaving me defenseless,
My trust torn apart.
Then slowly, you creep
Back into my mind
With soft words of love
And promises to be kind.
Then, you bring me flowers
When it's too late.
That's like putting icing
On a burnt cake.
I needed the flowers
When I knew you cared,
Not when you were no longer there.
I can't believe you would
Use my weakness
And misuse my love and kindness.
You took my weakness

Tanya "Trinity" Holland

And made it your weapon.
You manipulated my thoughts
And held me captive.
But now, I am going to take my weakness
And use it as my strength,
As I kindly and lovingly
Let You Go
Because my spirit is okay
With being alone.

2 Corinthians 12:9-10

"But He said to me, 'My grace is sufficient for you, for My power is made perfect in weakness.' Therefore, I will boast all the more gladly about my weaknesses, so that Christ's power may rest on me. That is why, for Christ's sake, I delight in weaknesses, in insults, in hardships, in persecutions, in difficulties. For when I am weak, then I am strong."

Tanya "Trinity" Holland

Living Will

As I stand over this thing
That was once called a relationship
And watch the rhythm slowly fade,
I put my hand upon the pulse—
Feeling the heart that used to
Pump love through my veins.
I put my hands upon that
Beautiful chest that holds that heart,
And I slowly begin to push
And push and push,
Hoping to revive some type of
Emotion in you.
I put my lips upon your mouth,
Praying I can breathe some type
Of life back into the lungs
That used to speak love and life
Into me.
Then, I inject your veins with
The epinephrine of exotic
Text messages
With half-naked pictures
To speed up your heart
And entice your flesh,
Just to get you back into my bed.
Then, I shock your heart
With my amazingly erotic lovemaking
And pump your body full of fluids,
As you are drenched in sweat.
Then, the rhythm starts to fade
And the pulse becomes weak
And you grow cold.
I try to put my hands
Upon your chest,
But you pull away.

Then, I try to put my lips on yours,
But you no longer want
Your lungs to be filled.
I seemed to have forgotten:
This relationship
Did not start with a
Living Will...

Tanya "Trinity" Holland

The Carpet

I went into this union,
Thinking it was forever
And that no man would put asunder,
But they should have also said
"No Woman."
Because she was the one
You allowed to pull the carpet
Out from under.
What God had brought together,
You allowed a wedge to divide
What God had solidified.
Because you chose to take the fruit
From the wrong tree,
And allowed your flesh
To conquer thee.
Which, in turn,
Devoured me.
But God's grace is sufficient;
He allowed a way for me,
Through His precious Son,
So that I can be free
From your iniquities.

Matthew 19:6

"So they are no longer two, but one flesh. Therefore, what God has joined together, let no one separate."

Repenting

Forgive me, Father,
For the crime
That I am about to commit:
Murder in the worst degree,
And for this, I must repent.
I know You wouldn't give me
More than I could bear,
So for this, I must say this prayer
To ask that You will take care
Of this life I cannot share.
Forgive me, Mother and Father,
For not allowing you to know
This part of my soul.
Forgive me, my family,
Because what lives within me
Will never be a part of
This family tree.
Now I lay me
Down on this cold bed,
As the drugs fill my veins
And cloud my head.
My body starts to shiver,
As my life grows dimmer.
Please forgive me, Father,
For it is done.
This heart wrenching decision
To take my unborn one.

1 John 1:9

"If we confess our sins, He is faithful and just and will forgive us our sins and purify us from all unrighteousness.'

Acts 3:19

"Repent, then, and turn to God, so that your sins may be wiped out, that times of refreshing may come from the Lord..."

Luke 15:10

"In the same way, I tell you, there is rejoicing in the presence of the angels of God over one sinner who repents."

Lost

To the world outside,
I am a strong woman.
To my world inside,
I'm a weak child
Still trapped inside the womb.
To the world outside,
I am fearless.
To my world inside,
I am foolish.
To the world outside,
I stand alone.
To my world inside,
I am all alone.
To the world outside,
I am a conqueror.
To my world inside,
I am a failure.
To the world outside,
I am driven.
To my world inside,
I am hidden.
To the world outside,
I hold my place.
To my world inside,
I have no face.
To the world outside,
I am
Independent, Strong,
Fearless, and Driven.
But to my world inside,
I AM LOST!

Drowning

I feel myself swimming
In an ocean
Filled with deep thoughts
Of depression
And swirling emotions,
But I'm finding it hard
To keep my head above the water.
And sometimes, the water takes over,
Then I feel myself drowning.
My body becomes numb,
And the darkness of the deep
Starts to succumb—
Pulling me deeper and deeper
Into the abyss.
I start fighting for air,
Wanting to feel the kiss
Of the sun on my face,
Hoping someone will come
To my rescue
Before my spirit leaves this place,
But there is no one in sight.
Then, my mind starts to wonder,
"Should I just give up this fight,
Or should I start to swim?"
But the aching in my body
Changes my mind again,
Reminding me what it was like
On the surface,
Dealing with life's purpose.
I look deep in my soul,
Searching for a meaning
To keep on living,
But the dark waters keep swallowing me.
Maybe I should just let go

And let my soul give way...
I'll no longer have to worry
About what will happen the next day.
No more heartache. No more pain.
No more disappointment.
Over and over again,
I start to lose consciousness
And ponder if I will be missed.
My life passes before me,
And I begin to realize this:
There are people who need me
To try and keep swimming...
To keep fighting...
To keep breathing...
But none of those people are here.
This battle is mine
To fight alone.
Then, a soft voice
Whispers in my ear,
"This world will be lost
Without you here."
Then, the waters become rough—
Something from the deep
Is lifting me up.
Then, I begin to fight;
I can feel the sunlight
On my face.
The sun is blinding,
Quickly reminding
That there is hope.
In spite of drowning,
My depression won't win.
Not this time.
Not again.
I choose to live
And not keep drowning.

Matthew 7:7

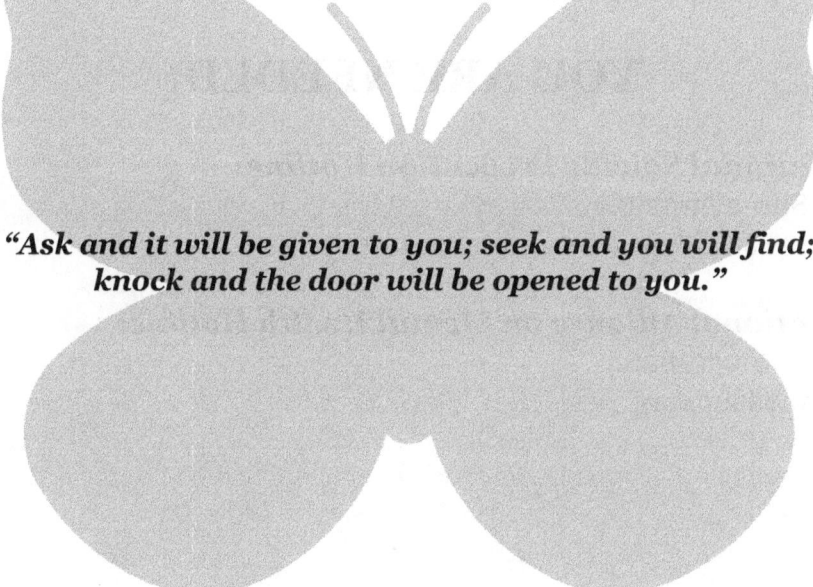

"Ask and it will be given to you; seek and you will find; knock and the door will be opened to you."

You Are Needed

If someone you know is suffering from depression, anxiety, PTSD, or a mental illness of any kind, remember: They are in the fight of their life. Love them. Be kind. Be patient. Be understanding. Assist them with seeking help. It's likely they don't even know they are drowning.

If you are suffering from the same, remember to love yourself because the pain you leave behind is much harder to bear than the pain you may be feeling right now. Never be afraid to reach out for help and support. Someone is waiting to assist you who has probably been right where you are.

YOU ARE NEEDED!

National Suicide Prevention Hotline:
1-800-273-8255
www.suicidepreventionlifeline.org

National Alliance on Mental Health Hotline:
1-800-950-6264
www.nami.org

Perfect

You put me on a pedestal,
And you shower me with gifts.
You take me to meet your Mama,
And to church to meet your pastor
When you really don't know
The whole me—
Let alone half of me.
And I'm afraid to tell you
Because of the judgment
That might fall.
When you look at me,
All you see is Perfection.
A thing of beauty...
A work of art
Like a Van Gogh
Or Michelangelo,
But I am far from perfect.
And I am so afraid to tell you
Because it will ruin it all,
And surely, my pedestal will fall.
Everyone has a past,
And mine wasn't so pretty.
And even though I left it there,
It's still a part of me.
As much as I want to be
The perfect woman for you,
I'm just not sure I can fill her shoes.
I pray you will understand
When I step down
From the pedestal you built
That I am just a woman
Full of past regrets and guilt—
And that I am far
From Perfect.

Tanya "Trinity" Holland

John 15:12, 16-17

"My command is this: Love each other as I have loved you. You did not choose Me, but I chose you and appointed you so that you might go and bear fruit—fruit that will last—and so that whatever you ask in My name the Father will give you. This is My command: Love each other."

Resilience

When she learned how to bounce back...

Tanya "Trinity" Holland

Rear View

I'm heading it off at the past
Because I promised myself
I wouldn't repeat it.
Always finding myself lost and defeated.
I'm taking a different fork
In the road of self-worth and work.
I'm slowing down at the yellow light
To look in both directions
Because you never know what's coming
From the left or the right.
I'm yielding into the flow
Of this new direction,
Making sure to take it slow
And make all the right corrections.
I will not pass unless it's on the left.
LORD knows if I pass on the right,
He will make sure to straighten my path.
So, I'm heading it off at my past
So that I don't repeat it;
Leaving it behind
So when I look in my rear view,
I can no longer see it...

More to Me

What you see isn't always
What you get.
Give it some time;
We just met.
I may look good today,
But I don't always look this way
Because some days,
I feel like wearing sweats
And putting my hair in a ponytail.
Other days,
I look fine as hell.
There is so much more to me
Than what you see.
You'll only get to see the real beauty
If you are willing to take that journey.
First impressions aren't much
To be desired.
Chemical reactions can often
Spark a fire.
But once that fire is out
And the smoke has cleared,
There isn't much left
But ash and tears.
Some fires don't have to burn so quick;
Fizzled out with nothing left
But a wick.
So, lets take some time
And put aside the pheromones
To see if this is something worth growin'.
I'm not trying to hold you down:
I'm trying to lift you up,
Keep your head above water,
Not letting you give up.
But you won't see that part of me

Tanya "Trinity" Holland

Because you can't see
Past this booty.
There is so much more to me
Than just the physical parts.
There is a spiritual side—
The one that's connected to my heart.
I don't want you to just
Make love to my body;
I want you to love my mind
And learn the things that
Make me happy,
'Cause there is so much more to me
Than what you see.
There is a person inside—
The one I don't always show
Because she likes to hide.
This side of me
Hides for a reason.
Every time she showed,
She suffered humiliation.
So, If you can get beyond
What you see,
You'll see there's more to me—
The me who wants, needs,
And gives love
But doesn't always get enough of.
So, slow your roll,
And maybe
You will get to know
There is More to Me.

Nations

People often ask me,
"What's your nationality?"
So, my answer to them is this:
"When you look at me,
You see nations
Because my ancestors birthed nations.
Nations of people who came unto them
And stole their countries,
And then came into them
And they birthed nations.
My son's wife will birth nations
Because nations live within them.
And when two people, who were "Loving"
Became wrong,
We still became a nation
Because love conquers all.
I don't need Ancestry.com
To know my ancestry
Because a nation of my ancestors
Taught me who they were.
So, you must be too blind to see
That this nation
Is built upon nations and
The beautiful colors of people
Who live within it.
And you are also too deaf to hear
The continuous cries to end racism
Of people who live in fear.
And your ignorance shows
Because you do not understand
That we are one nation
Full of nationalities.
But divided,
We cannot stand.

Tanya "Trinity" Holland

Tragically Beautiful

They say, "Beauty is in the eye of the beholder."
I say, "Beauty is held in the eye of the tragedy."
The tragedy of this so-called life
That beats her into submission
With no reason or disposition.
This beautiful tragedy
That makes her beautiful,
Through all that has torn her apart
And driven her dreams into the cracks
Of the walls of this cell called 'depression.'
The war wounds and scars,
The battle-torn body
That ravages with the pain
Of this beautiful tragedy.
Beauty is held in the eye of the beholder,
But hold her
Because this tragedy
Is way too much for her to bear.
Her strength wavers at the thought
Of dealing with the everyday weight
Of this tragic life.
All the things that have been thrown at her
Because she is "the strong one."
The ones who have taken advantage of her
Kind and giving heart, only to be
Tragically broken
Because her beauty is held
In the eyes of her tragedy.
Because she is
Tragically Beautiful.

Allowance

I allowed you into my heart,
And you penetrated my soul.
I allowed you to break down walls
That were a lifetime deep.
I allowed you to make me feel
Ugly, fat, and weak.
I allowed you to make me feel stupid
Whenever I opened my mouth to speak.
I allowed you to make me feel less elegant
When you would comment on the way I dressed.
You made me feel ignorant,
Just by the look on your face,
Because I am nothing to you
But an embarrassment.
I allowed you to come into my life,
Feeling that you could make me complete.
Now, I'm sitting here
Feeling nothing but defeat.
I allowed you to make me feel undesirable,
And when I'm right here in front of you,
I allowed you to make me feel invisible.
I allowed you to make me feel
That I didn't deserve
To be treated like a human.
For you, I am only meant to serve.
I allowed you to shut me down
When I was trying to make a point.
No longer feeling like I had a choice,
Let alone a voice.
I allowed you
To make me feel like
My pain didn't count,
Because after what you've been through,
Yours was much worse

Tanya "Trinity" Holland

Without a doubt.
I allowed you to make me feel
Weak and worthless
And unworthy of kindness.
Well, today—right this minute—
I'm taking back my heart, mind, and spirit
To allow the dynamic woman
Whom God created,
To heal and grow and not be jaded.
I am no longer giving you
ALLOWANCE.

Give It to Me

Give it to Me,
And I will put it in my hands
And make it safe again.

Give it to Me,
And I will put it in my hands
And wrap it in silver, gold, and diamonds
And make it beautiful again.

Give it to Me,
And I will put it in my hands
And take the glue
And make it whole again.

Give it to Me,
And I will put it in my hands
And make it feel loved again.

Give it to Me,
And I will put it in my hands
And help it stand upright again.

Give it to Me,
And I will put it in front of Me
And teach it to love and trust again.

Give it to Me,
And I will put it in the sun,
Give it some water,
And let it grow again.

Give it to Me,
And I will feed and nourish it
So that it will no longer feel hungry or thirsty again.

Tanya "Trinity" Holland

Give it to Me,
And I will take it in my arms
And never let it go,
So that it knows that I am
Always here.

Give it to Me,
For I am it's Savior, Comforter,
Lover, Teacher, and Creator—
And I will never fail!

Isaiah 41:10

"So do not fear, for I am with you; do not be dismayed, for I am your God. I will strengthen you and help you; I will uphold you with My righteous right hand."

The Mourning

When you mourn the death of yourself,
Not particularly the death of your soul
But simply the death of your former self,
You mourn that death as if you actually died.
You cry, scream, get angry, and deny
That this could possibly be.
You still try to hold on to every piece
Of the person that once was you.
You are still that person...
Just not the same.
Change is difficult.
You fight it with everything you have.
You will kick, bite, scratch, and punch,
But the new you will just
Hold and comfort the old you
Until you are consoled and accepting of the new you.
Even after you have surrendered,
It still doesn't feel real.
Confusion sets in,
But the darkness is broken by the light
Of the New You.

Ephesians 4:22-24

"You were taught, with regard to your former way of life, to put off your old self, which is being corrupted by its deceitful desires; to be made new in the attitude of your minds; and to put on the new self, created to be like God in true righteousness and holiness."

Tanya "Trinity" Holland

Resilience

I can't look back;
I can only look ahead
Because this is the new me.
Unbreakable, Unstoppable,
Renewed and Restored,
Undeniably determined
To reconstruct what was destroyed
And to replete what was devoid.
Nonrefundable.
Nonreturnable.
The past has left the building.
There will be no encore.
Exchanging bad memories
With better experiences…
These old dreams,
Brought back to life
By resurrecting the gift in me.
There is no reverse in my driveshaft
Because I am driven.
There are no U-turns on my path
On this journey to greatness.
Like the phoenix that rose from the ashes,
The Holy Spirit sparks the flames
Of these once dead dreams.
They will shine with such brilliance
Fueled by
RESILIENCE.

Matthew 5:14-16

"You are the light of the world. A town built on a hill cannot be hidden. Neither do people light a lamp and put it under a bowl. Instead, they put it on its stand, and it gives light to everyone in the house. In the same way, let your light shine before others, that they may see your good deeds and glorify your Father in Heaven."

James 1:12

"Blessed is the one who perseveres under trial because, having stood the test, that person will receive the crown of life that the Lord has promised to those who love Him."

For anyone who has struggled with addiction of any kind, battled with PTSD, or endured a life of trauma, the following poem is for you.

Madness

Emptiness.
Deep within me...emptiness.
My soul is empty,
But my mind is full—
Full of empty thoughts.
Self-pity, self-loathing,
Telling myself I'm not worthy.
So many sins, so many mistakes,
So many bad decisions,
So many heartaches.
Emptiness.
Feeling nothing...emptiness.
My soul is empty.
My mind echoes
With painful thoughts and memories
That bounce around like razors in my brain,
Constantly reminding me
That I could never be worthy,
For what have I ever done
To be worthy?
Emptiness.
Emptying out my crowded mind.
My soul is empty.
My heart is full of bitterness
From all the disappointments
Of empty relationships.
Looking for fulfillment
In emptiness is
Madness.
Empty...Emptiness.

Tanya "Trinity" Holland

My soul is empty.
Crying out to a deaf world
Filled with egotistical, narrow-minded,
Superficial, empty people
Shouting, "I AM EMPTY!"
Emptiness.
Lack of substance.
Less than nothing.
Not half-full;
Not even half-empty.
Just EMPTY.
Trying to fill this emptiness
With worldly substances
And temporary fixes is
MADNESS.
Emptiness.
My soul is empty.
Exhausted, tired, no longer
Having the will.
Weak.
Empty.
Lost.
Finally finding myself
On the ground
On my knees
With my head down and my arms outstretched,
Saying to the only One
Who would listen,
"I am tired of being empty!
I surrender! I give up!
I can no longer try to fill the
Emptiness.
I give it unto You—
The only One who can make me whole.
Father God,
Jesus my Savior,

I am empty.
I am ready.
I am worthy
Of Your love
So that I will no longer feel
EMPTY.

Matthew 6:33

"But seek first His kingdom and His righteousness, and all these things will be given to you as well."

About the Author

Tanya "Trinity" Holland is a nurse by profession, but writing and poetry are her art. She started writing at the young age of 14 as an outlet for a troubled home life. During her teen and young adult years, she studied and performed in the theater and was inducted into the Youth Thespian Society while in high school. Acting is one of the things that inspired her love for writing.

Tanya's recent poetry spans over 20 years. She has also performed her art as Spoken Word in many venues, including Trenton, New Jersey; Philadelphia, Pennsylvania; and Orlando, Florida. "Trinity" was also an opening act for well-known comedians Lisa Lampanelli and Will-E Robo.

Love, Lessons, & Resilience is Tanya's first published book of her poetry.

Tanya "Trinity" Holland

www.ingramcontent.com/pod-product-compliance
Lightning Source LLC
Chambersburg PA
CBHW070655050426
42451CB00008B/366